Classic
BALTI

Classic BALTI

Fast and delicious stir-fry curries

SHEHZAD HUSAIN

UNIVERSAL

First published by Ultimate Editions in 1996

© 1996 Anness Publishing Limited

Ultimate Editions is an imprint of
Anness Publishing Limited
Boundary Row Studios
1 Boundary Row
London SE1 8HP

This edition distributed in Canada by Book Express
an imprint of Raincoast Books Distribution Limited

ISBN 1 86035 175 1

Publisher Joanna Lorenz
Senior Cookery Editor Linda Fraser
Cookery Editor Anne Hildyard
Designer Nigel Partridge
Illustrations Madeleine David
Photographers David Armstrong
Food for photography Shehzad Husain
Jacket photography Amanda Heywood

Typeset by MC Typeset Ltd, Rochester, Kent

Printed in Singapore

For all recipes, quantities are given in both metric and imperial measures, and, where appropriate,
measures are also given in standard cups and spoons. Follow one set, but not a mixture,
because they are not interchangeable.

Pictures on frontispiece, pages 8 and 9: Christine Osborne Pictures
Picture on page 7: Zefa Pictures Ltd

CONTENTS

INTRODUCTION

There can rarely have been a culinary phenomenon quite like the success of Balti cooking in the last few years. From being quite unheard of and unknown, Balti has changed the menus of Indian-style restaurants, sweeping all other dishes before it. Unlike some of the more elaborate popular recipes found in oriental restaurants, though, Balti has also spread into the home. Because it is so simple, quick and easy, Balti is the perfect style of cooking for people who love Indian-style food but don't have hours to spare to prepare it. This book shows you how easy it is to make Balti food.

What is Balti? In essence, it is a style of curry that is cooked quickly on the top of the stove, in a pan, using a stir-fry technique. Originating in northern Pakistan, in a mountainous and isolated state called Baltistan, Balti is a centuries-old cuisine, combining Tibetan influence with Kashmiri-style spicing. However, because it is so easy to do in a western kitchen, Balti really is ideal for today's busy cooks. They can produce aromatic, fresh, spicy and very tasty dishes, like Balti Butter Chicken and Balti Prawns in Hot Sauce, in minutes.

The distinctive characteristic of Balti is the cooking pan, known as a *karahi*. An authentic Balti pan is a cast-iron, two-handled dish with a rounded bottom. However, Asian shops now sell Balti pans in a variety of other metals and lots of different sizes, along with as wooden or metal stands,

so you can bring the pans to the table to serve. The pan needs to be sturdy enough to withstand the high cooking temperatures and sizzling oils used in Balti cooking. A sturdy wok or a deep, rounded frying pan can be substituted, if you don't want to buy a special pan. It has to be said, though, that using the real thing to cook in, adds to the enjoyment of Balti cooking. A choice of pan sizes – such as one 20cm/8in and one 30cm/12in – makes life easier. You can cook small quantities and start off stir-fry mixtures in the smaller one, as well as using it to make individual portions or accompaniments, such as Spicy Balti Potatoes, and the bigger karahi can be used for complete Balti recipes for four or more people.

The other specialist cooking vessel used is the *tava*. This flat, cast-iron frying pan is used for cooking some breads and for roasting spices – any sturdy frying pan can be used instead.

A food processor or blender is a great labour-saving tool and will be invaluable for making pastes and puréeing ingredients. Whole spices can be freshly ground the traditional way, using a pestle and mortar; or, if you have one, a coffee grinder is effortless and efficient. It is best to keep a grinder specially for grinding spices to avoid affecting the flavour of your coffee. Any other

Houseboats on the river in the late evening sun (right).

equipment, such as heavy-based saucepans, wooden spoons, mixing bowls, sharp knives, a chopping board, sieve and rolling pin, will probably be in your kitchen already.

Because Balti is a very quick cooking method, choose the best quality ingredients: the crispest vegetables; lean and tender meat and poultry, and fish and shellfish that taste of the sea. Take advantage of produce at its seasonal best and full of flavour and

don't be afraid to substitute other seasonally available ingredients for those specified in the recipes. Balti has no strict rules and you can make your own combinations.

To achieve the authentic Balti taste, use fresh herbs and freshly ground spices. Most can be purchased from Asian shops and supermarkets. Remember that whole spices keep their flavour for longer than ready-ground ones, as well as tasting much

dried and fresh chillies. Some brands and varieties are much hotter than others, so experiment with quantities, adding less than specified in the recipe, if you like. There is no law that says that Balti dishes have to be hot – it really is just a matter of taste. After preparing and chopping chillies, wash your hands thoroughly with soap and water and avoid touching your face, especially your lips and eyes, for a good while afterwards.

Garam masala is a blend of spices that does not need cooking and is simply sprinkled on to cooked dishes at the last minute. It's particularly useful for short-cooked Balti dishes, and, though ready-made mixtures can be bought, home-made garam masala has the best flavour.

Vendors preparing strings of hot spicy sausages for Baltistan-style hot dogs at an open-air market (left); carefully arranged rows of fresh vegetables in a street market in Pakistan (above).

better to start with. Store spices in cool, dark, dry conditions, in airtight containers.

Many different spices are used in this book and it is the combination of spices that gives Balti cooking its unique, aromatic flavour. It is important to use spices judiciously; too much or too little of one spice can completely alter the balance of a dish. But it is also important that you experiment with spices, increasing and decreasing them to suit your own taste. This is especially true of chilli powder and

---

HOME-MADE GARAM MASALA

4 × 2.5cm/1in cinnamon sticks

3 cloves

3 black peppercorns

2 black cardamom pods, husks removed

10ml/2 tsp black cumin seeds

Grind the spices together in a coffee grinder or with a pestle in a mortar until they are quite a fine powder.

PRAWNS WITH POMEGRANATE SEEDS

K ing prawns are the best ones for this dish. It makes an impressive appetizer for a dinner party, and is delicious served with a mixed salad.

INGREDIENTS

5ml/1 tsp crushed garlic
5ml/1 tsp sliced fresh root ginger
5ml/1 tsp coarsely ground pomegranate seeds
5ml/1 tsp ground coriander
5ml/1 tsp salt
5ml/1 tsp chilli powder
30ml/2 tbsp tomato purée
60ml/4 tbsp water
45ml/3 tbsp chopped fresh coriander
30ml/2 tbsp corn oil
12 large cooked prawns
1 onion, sliced into rings

Serves 4–6

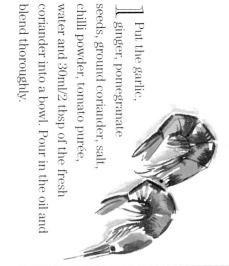

1 Put the garlic, ginger, pomegranate seeds, ground coriander, salt, chilli powder, tomato purée, water and 30ml/2 tbsp of the fresh coriander into a bowl. Pour in the oil and blend thoroughly.

2 Peel the prawns. Using a sharp knife, make a small slit at the back of each prawn, then gently open them out to make a butterfly shape.

3 Add the prawns to the spice mixture, coating them well. Cover and leave to marinate for about 2 hours.

4 Cut four squares of foil, each about 20 × 20 cm/8 × 8 in. Preheat the oven to 230°C/450°F/Gas 8. Place three prawns and a few onion rings on each square of foil, garnishing them with a little fresh coriander, and fold up into little packages. Bake the prawns for about 12–15 minutes and open up the foil packages to serve.

A mixed salad (TOP) is delicious with Prawns with Pomegranate Seeds and Grilled Prawns

GRILLED PRAWNS

P rawns are delicious grilled, especially when they are flavoured with spices.

INGREDIENTS

60ml/4 tbsp lemon juice
5ml/1 tsp salt
5ml/1 tsp chilli powder
1 garlic clove, crushed
7.5ml/1½ tsp soft light brown sugar
45ml/3 tbsp corn oil
30ml/2 tbsp chopped fresh coriander
18 large peeled, cooked prawns
1 fresh green chilli, sliced
1 tomato, sliced
1 small onion, cut into rings
lemon wedges, to garnish

Serves 4–6

1 Combine the lemon juice, salt, chilli powder, garlic, sugar, corn oil and fresh coriander in a bowl. Add the prawns, coating them well. Cover and leave to marinate for about 1 hour.

2 Place the green chilli, tomato slices and onion rings in a flameproof dish. Add the prawn mixture and cook under a preheated very hot grill for about 10–15 minutes, basting several times. Serve at once, garnished with the lemon wedges.

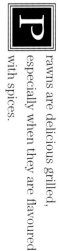

CHICKEN AND ALMOND SOUP

T his soup makes an excellent appetizer and, served with Naan Bread, will also make a satisfying lunch or supper dish.

INGREDIENTS

75g/3oz/6 tbsp unsalted butter

1 leek, chopped

2.5ml/½ tsp sliced fresh root ginger

75g/3oz/1 cup ground almonds

5ml/1 tsp salt

2.5ml/½ tsp crushed black peppercorns

1 fresh green chilli, chopped

115g/4oz chicken, skinned, boned
and cubed

1 carrot, sliced

50g/2oz/½ cup frozen peas

15ml/1 tbsp chopped fresh coriander

450ml/¾ pint/scant 2 cups water

250ml/8fl oz/1 cup single cream

4 fresh coriander sprigs, to garnish

SERVES 4

1 Melt the butter in a large karahi or deep round-bottomed frying pan and sauté the leek with the ginger until soft.

2 Lower the heat and add the ground almonds, salt, peppercorns, chilli, chicken, carrot and peas. Fry for about 10 minutes or until the chicken is completely cooked, stirring constantly. Add the chopped fresh coriander.

3 Remove the pan from the heat and allow to cool slightly. Transfer the mixture to a food processor or blender and process for about 1½ minutes. Pour in the water and blend for a further 30 seconds.

4 Pour the puréed mixture back into the karahi or frying pan and bring slowly to the boil, stirring occasionally. Once the soup has boiled, lower the heat and gradually stir in the single cream. Cook the soup, without bringing to the boil, for a further 2 minutes, stirring occasionally, until the cream is just heated through.

5 To serve, transfer the soup to warmed individual bowls, garnish each one with a fresh coriander sprig and serve immediately.

SPICY CHICKEN AND MUSHROOM SOUP

T his creamy chicken soup makes a hearty meal for a winter's night when served with hot garlic bread.

INGREDIENTS

225g/8oz chicken, skinned and boned
75g/3oz/6 tbsp unsalted butter
½ garlic clove, crushed
5ml/1 tsp garam masala
5ml/1 tsp crushed black peppercorns
5ml/1 tsp salt
1.5ml/¼ tsp ground nutmeg
1 leek, sliced
75g/3oz/1 cup mushrooms, sliced
50g/2oz/⅓ cup sweetcorn
300ml/½ pint/1¼ cups water
250ml/8fl oz/1 cup single cream
15ml/1 tbsp chopped fresh coriander
5ml/1 tsp crushed dried red chillies
(optional), to garnish

SERVES 4

1 Using a sharp knife, cut the chicken pieces into very fine strips. Melt the butter in a saucepan and add the garlic and garam masala. Lower the heat and add the peppercorns, salt and nutmeg. Finally, add the chicken, leek, mushrooms and sweetcorn and cook for 5–7 minutes or until the chicken is cooked through, stirring constantly.

2 Remove the saucepan from the heat and allow the chicken mixture to cool slightly. Transfer three-quarters of the mixture to a food processor or blender. Add the water and process for about 1 minute until smooth.

3 Stir the purée back into the saucepan with the rest of the mixture and bring to the boil over a moderate heat. Lower the heat and stir in the cream.

4 Add the fresh coriander, then taste for seasoning. Serve hot, garnished with the crushed red chillies, if using.

CHICKEN KOFTA BALTI WITH PANEER

This rather unusual appetizer looks most elegant when served in small individual karahis. Serve it as a starter for a dinner party.

INGREDIENTS

FOR THE KOFTAS

450g/1lb chicken, skinned, boned and cubed

1 garlic clove, crushed

5ml/1 tsp sliced fresh root ginger

7.5ml/1½ tsp ground coriander

7.5ml/1½ tsp chilli powder

2.5ml/½ tsp ground fenugreek

1.5ml/¼ tsp turmeric

5ml/1 tsp salt

30ml/2 tbsp chopped fresh coriander

2 fresh green chillies, chopped

600ml/1 pint/2½ cups water

corn oil, for frying

FOR THE PANEER MIXTURE

1 onion, sliced

175g/6oz paneer, cubed

1 green pepper, seeded and cut into strips

1 red pepper, seeded and cut into strips

175g/6oz/1 cup sweetcorn

mint sprigs and 1 dried red chilli, crushed (optional), to garnish

SERVES 6

1 To make the koftas, put the chicken, garlic, ginger, ground coriander, chilli powder, fenugreek, turmeric, salt, fresh coriander, chillies and water into a saucepan. Bring to the boil slowly over a moderate heat and cook until all the liquid has evaporated.

2 Remove the pan from the heat and allow to cool slightly. Put the mixture into a food processor or blender and process for 2 minutes, stopping the machine once or twice to loosen the mixture with a wooden spoon or a rubber spatula.

3 Transfer the mixture to a large bowl with a wooden spoon. Taking a little of the mixture at a time, shape it into small balls with your hands. You should be able to make about 12 koftas.

4 Heat the oil in a karahi or deep round-bottomed frying pan over a high heat. Turn down the heat slightly and place the koftas carefully in the oil. Stir them around gently so that they cook evenly.

5 When the koftas are lightly browned, remove them from the oil with a slotted spoon and drain on kitchen paper. Set aside while you cook the paneer.

6 To make the paneer mixture, heat the oil remaining in the karahi, add the onion, paneer, green and red pepper strips and sweetcorn and flash fry over a high heat for 3 minutes, until cooked.

7 Using a slotted spoon, divide the paneer mixture evenly among 6 individual karahis. Add 2 koftas to each serving and garnish with mint sprigs and a sprinkling of crushed red chilli, if using.

BALTI CHICKEN WITH LENTILS

This recipe has a rather unusual combination of flavours, but it is well worth trying. The mango powder gives a delicious tangy flavour to the finished dish.

INGREDIENTS
75g/3oz/½ cup chana dhal (split yellow lentils)
60ml/4 tbsp corn oil
2 leeks, chopped
6 dried red chillies
4 curry leaves
5ml/1 tsp mustard seeds
10ml/2 tsp mango powder
2 tomatoes, chopped
2.5ml/½ tsp chilli powder
5ml/1 tsp ground coriander
5ml/1 tsp salt
450g/1lb chicken, skinned, boned and cubed
15ml/1 tbsp chopped fresh coriander

SERVES 4–6

COOK'S TIP
Chana dhal is available from Asian stores. However, split yellow peas from delicatessens and supermarkets make a good substitute.

---

1 Wash the lentils carefully under cold running water and remove any stones or pieces of grit.

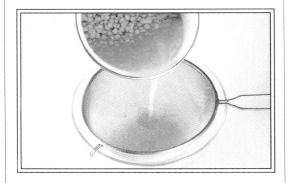

2 Put the lentils into a saucepan with enough water to cover and boil for about 10 minutes until they are soft but not mushy. Drain and set aside in a bowl.

3 Heat the oil in a medium karahi or deep round-bottomed frying pan. Lower the heat slightly and add the leeks, dried red chillies, curry leaves and mustard seeds. Stir-fry gently for a few minutes.

4 Add the mango powder, tomatoes, chilli powder, ground coriander, salt and chicken and stir-fry for 7–10 minutes.

5 Mix in the cooked lentils and fry for a further 2 minutes, or until the chicken is thoroughly cooked.

6 Garnish with the fresh coriander and serve at once.

BALTI CHICKEN PASANDA

asanda dishes are firm favourites in Pakistan and now they are becoming so in the West.

INGREDIENTS

60ml/4 tbsp Greek yogurt

2.5ml/½ tsp black cumin seeds

4 cardamom pods

6 whole black peppercorns

10ml/2 tsp garam masala

2.5cm/1in piece cinnamon stick

15ml/1 tbsp ground almonds

1 garlic clove, crushed

5ml/1 tsp sliced fresh root ginger

5ml/1 tsp chilli powder

5ml/1 tsp salt

675g/1½lb chicken, skinned, boned and cubed

75ml/5 tbsp corn oil

2 onions, diced

3 fresh green chillies, chopped

30ml/2 tbsp chopped fresh coriander

120ml/4fl oz/½ cup single cream

SERVES 4

1 Mix the yogurt, cumin seeds, cardamom pods, peppercorns, garam masala, cinnamon stick, ground almonds, garlic, ginger, chilli powder and salt in a medium bowl. Add the chicken pieces, cover and leave to marinate for about 2 hours.

2 Heat the oil in a large karahi or deep round-bottomed frying pan. Add the onions and fry for 2–3 minutes.

3 Add the chicken mixture and stir until it is thoroughly combined with the onions.

4 Cook the chicken and spice mixture over a moderate heat, stirring occasionally, for 12–15 minutes, or until the sauce is thickened and the chicken pieces are cooked through.

5 Add the green chillies and fresh coriander, pour in the cream and bring to the boil. Serve garnished with more coriander, if wished.

BALTI CHILLI CHICKEN

Hot and spicy is the best way of describing this Balti dish. The aroma of the fresh chillies cooking is truly mouth-watering!

INGREDIENTS
75ml/5 tbsp corn oil
8 large fresh green chillies, slit
2.5ml/½ tsp mixed onion and cumin seeds
4 curry leaves
5ml/1 tsp sliced fresh root ginger
5ml/1 tsp chilli powder
5ml/1 tsp ground coriander
1 garlic clove, crushed
5ml/1 tsp salt
2 onions, chopped
675g/1½lb chicken, skinned, boned and cubed
15ml/1 tbsp lemon juice
15ml/1 tbsp roughly chopped fresh mint
15ml/1 tbsp roughly chopped fresh coriander
8–10 cherry tomatoes

SERVES 4–6

1 Heat the oil in a deep round-bottomed frying pan or a karahi. Lower the heat slightly, add the slit green chillies and fry until the skins start to change colour. Remove the chillies to a plate.

2 Add the onion and cumin seeds, curry leaves, ginger, chilli powder, ground coriander, garlic, salt and onions to the pan and fry for a few seconds, stirring the mixture constantly.

3 Add the chicken pieces and stir-fry for 7–10 minutes, or until the chicken is cooked right through.

4 Sprinkle the lemon juice over the chicken and add the mint and coriander.

5 Add the cherry tomatoes and return the chillies to the pan. Heat through and serve with Naan Bread or Parathas.

BALTI BUTTER CHICKEN

Butter Chicken is one of the most popular Balti chicken dishes, especially in the West. Cooked in butter, with aromatic spices, cream and almonds, this mild dish will be enjoyed by everyone. Serve with Colourful Pullao Rice.

INGREDIENTS

150ml/¼ pint/⅔ cup natural yogurt
50g/2oz/½ cup ground almonds
7.5ml/1½ tsp chilli powder
1.5ml/¼ tsp crushed bay leaves
1.5ml/¼ tsp ground cloves
1.5ml/¼ tsp ground cinnamon
5ml/1 tsp garam masala
4 green cardamom pods
5ml/1 tsp sliced fresh root ginger
1 garlic clove, crushed
400g/14oz/2 cups canned tomatoes
7.5ml/1½ tsp salt
1kg/2¼lb chicken, skinned, boned and cubed
75g/3oz/6 tbsp butter
15ml/1 tbsp corn oil
2 onions, sliced
30ml/2 tbsp chopped fresh coriander
60ml/4 tbsp single cream
coriander sprigs, to garnish

SERVES 4–6

1 Put the yogurt, ground almonds, chilli powder, bay leaves, cloves, cinnamon, garam masala, cardamom, ginger, garlic, tomatoes and salt into a bowl and blend.

2 Put the chicken into a large bowl and pour over the yogurt mixture. Set aside.

3 Melt the butter with the oil in a karahi or deep round-bottomed frying pan. Add the onions and fry for about 3 minutes.

4 Add the chicken mixture and stir-fry for 7–10 minutes.

5 Stir about half of the fresh coriander into the chicken mixture and mix well.

6 Pour over the cream and stir in well. Bring to the boil. Serve garnished with the remaining chopped coriander and coriander sprigs.

COOK'S TIP
You can replace the natural yogurt with Greek-style yogurt to obtain a richer and creamier flavour.

BALTI POUSSINS IN TAMARIND SAUCE

The chillies make this a quite hot Balti dish. Its subtle, sweet and sour flavour is due to the addition of the tamarind paste.

INGREDIENTS
60ml/4 tbsp tomato ketchup
15ml/1 tbsp tamarind paste
60ml/4 tbsp water
7.5ml/1½ tsp chilli powder
7.5ml/1½ tsp salt
15ml/1 tbsp sugar
7.5ml/1½ tsp sliced fresh root ginger
1½ garlic cloves, crushed
30ml/2 tbsp desiccated coconut
30ml/2 tbsp sesame seeds
5ml/1 tsp poppy seeds
5ml/1 tsp ground cumin
7.5ml/1½ tsp ground coriander
2 × 450g/1lb poussins, skinned and cut
into 6–8 pieces each
75ml/5 tbsp corn oil
8 curry leaves
2.5ml/½ tsp onion seeds
3 large dried red chillies
2.5ml/½ tsp fenugreek seeds
10–12 cherry tomatoes
45ml/3 tbsp chopped fresh coriander
2 fresh green chillies, chopped

SERVES 4–6

1 Put the tomato ketchup, tamarind paste and water into a large bowl and blend together with a fork until they are thoroughly combined.

2 Add the chilli powder, salt, sugar, ginger, garlic, coconut, sesame and poppy seeds, ground cumin and ground coriander to the mixture.

3 Add the poussin pieces and stir until they are well coated with the spice mixture. Set aside.

4 Heat the oil in a deep round-bottomed frying pan or a large karahi. Add the curry leaves, onion seeds, red chillies and fenugreek seeds and fry for 1 minute.

5 Lower the heat to moderate and add the poussin pieces with their sauce and stir well. Simmer for about 12–15 minutes, or until the poussin is thoroughly cooked.

6 Add the tomatoes, fresh coriander and green chillies, and serve with Colourful Pullao Rice if wished.

BALTI CHICKEN WITH VEGETABLES

In this recipe the chicken and vegetables are cut into strips which makes the finished dish look particularly attractive.

INGREDIENTS
60ml/4 tbsp corn oil
2 onions, sliced
4 garlic cloves, thickly sliced
450g/1lb chicken breast, skinned, boned and cut into strips
5ml/1 tsp salt
30ml/2 tbsp lime juice
3 fresh green chillies, chopped
2 carrots, cut into batons
2 potatoes, cut into 1cm/½in strips
1 courgette, cut into batons
lime slices, chopped fresh coriander and 2 fresh green chillies, cut into strips (optional), to garnish

SERVES 4–6

1 Heat the oil in a large karahi or deep round-bottomed frying pan. Lower the heat slightly, add the onions and fry until lightly browned.

2 Add half of the garlic slices and fry for a few seconds, then add the chicken strips and salt. Cook, stirring, until all the moisture in the pan has evaporated and the chicken is lightly browned.

3 Add the lime juice, green chillies, carrots, potatoes and courgettes to the pan. Turn up the heat and add the remaining garlic and stir-fry for about 7–10 minutes, or until the chicken is cooked through and the vegetables are just tender.

4 Transfer to a serving dish and garnish with the lime slices, fresh coriander and green chilli strips, if using.

SWEET AND SOUR BALTI CHICKEN

This dish combines a sweet and sour flavour with a creamy texture. It is delicious served with Colourful Pullao Rice or Naan Bread.

INGREDIENTS

45ml/3 tbsp tomato purée
30ml/2 tbsp Greek yogurt
7.5ml/1½ tsp garam masala
5ml/1 tsp chilli powder
1 garlic clove, crushed
30ml/2 tbsp mango chutney
5ml/1 tsp salt
2.5ml/½ tsp sugar (optional)
60ml/4 tbsp corn oil
675g/1½lb chicken, skinned, boned and cubed
150ml/¼ pint/⅔ cup water
2 fresh green chillies, chopped
30ml/2 tbsp chopped fresh coriander
30ml/2 tbsp single cream

SERVES 4

1 Put the tomato purée and Greek yogurt into a bowl (*left*), and add the garam masala, chilli powder, garlic, mango chutney, salt and sugar, if using. Stir until they are thoroughly mixed together.

2 Heat the oil in a deep round-bottomed frying pan or a large karahi. Lower the heat slightly and pour in the spice mixture. Bring to the boil and cook for about 2 minutes, stirring occasionally.

3 Add the chicken pieces and ... until they are well coated. Add the water to thin the sauce slightly. Continue cooking for 5–7 minutes, or until the chicken is tender.

4 Add half of the fresh chillies, half of the fresh coriander and the cream, and cook for a further 2 minutes, until the chicken is cooked through. Transfer to a warmed serving dish and garnish with the remaining chillies and coriander.

KHARA MASALA CHICKEN

Whole spices (*khara*) are used in this recipe, giving it a wonderfully rich flavour. This is a dry dish so it is best served with a raita and parathas.

INGREDIENTS

1.5ml/¼ tsp mustard seeds
1.5ml/¼ tsp each fennel and onion seeds
2 curry leaves
2.5ml/½ tsp crushed dried red chillies
2.5ml/½ tsp white cumin seeds
1.5ml/¼ tsp fenugreek seeds
2.5ml/½ tsp crushed pomegranate seeds
5ml/1 tsp salt
5ml/1 tsp sliced fresh root ginger
3 garlic cloves, sliced
60ml/4 tbsp corn oil
4 large fresh green chillies, slit
1 large onion, sliced
1 tomato, sliced
675g/1½lb chicken, skinned, boned and cubed
chopped fresh coriander, to garnish

SERVES 4

1 Mix together the mustard, fennel and onion seeds, curry leaves, crushed red chillies, cumin seeds, fenugreek seeds, crushed pomegranate seeds and salt in a large bowl, then add the ginger and garlic.

2 Heat the oil in a medium karahi or deep round-bottomed frying pan and stir in the spice mixture and green chillies. Add the onion and cook over a moderate heat, stirring occasionally for 5–7 minutes until the onion is soft and translucent.

3 Add the tomato and chicken pieces to the karahi and cook over a moderate heat for about 7 minutes, or until the chicken is cooked through and the sauce has thickened and reduced.

4 Stir the tomato and chicken mixture together thoroughly and continue cooking over a gentle heat for a further 3–5 minutes, until most of the sauce has reduced. Garnish the chicken with chopped fresh coriander and serve immediately.

BALTI FRIED FISH

D o not cut the fish pieces too small or they will tend to break up during cooking. The chillies can be omitted, if you like.

INGREDIENTS
675g/1½lb cod, or any other firm
white fish
1 onion, sliced
15ml/1 tbsp lemon juice
5ml/1 tsp salt
1 garlic clove, crushed
7.5ml/1½ tsp garam masala
30ml/2 tbsp chopped fresh coriander
5ml/1tsp crushed dried red chillies
2 tomatoes
30ml/2 tbsp cornflour
150ml/¼ pint/⅔ cup corn oil

SERVES 4–6

1 Skin the fish, cut it into even-size cubes and place them in a bowl. Cover and chill in the fridge.

2 Put the onion into a bowl and add the lemon juice, salt, garlic, garam masala, fresh coriander and crushed red chillies. Mix together well, then set aside.

3 Peel the tomatoes by dropping them into boiling water for a few seconds. Remove with a slotted spoon and gently peel off the skins. Chop the tomatoes roughly and add to the onion mixture in the bowl.

4 Put the onion and tomato mixture into a food processor or blender and process for about 30 seconds.

5 Remove the fish from the fridge. Pour the puréed mixture over the fish pieces and stir together well. Add the cornflour and mix again until the fish pieces are thoroughly coated.

6 Heat the oil in a deep round-bottomed frying pan or a karahi. Lower the heat slightly and add the fish pieces, a few at a time. Turn them gently with a slotted spoon as they will break easily. Cook for about 5 minutes until the fish is lightly browned.

7 Remove the fish pieces from the pan and drain on kitchen paper to absorb any excess oil. Cover the cooked fish and keep warm while you fry the remaining fish. This dish is delicious served with Apricot Chutney and parathas.

CHUNKY FISH BALTI WITH PEPPERS

dding a selection of peppers in as many different colours as possible makes this a very attractive and flavourful dish.

INGREDIENTS
450g/1lb cod, or any other firm white fish
7.5ml/1½ tsp ground cumin
10ml/2 tsp mango powder
5ml/1 tsp ground coriander
2.5ml/½ tsp chilli powder
5ml/1 tsp salt
5ml/1 tsp grated fresh root ginger
45ml/3 tbsp cornflour
150ml/¼ pint/⅔ cup corn oil
1 each green, orange and red peppers,
seeded and cut into chunks
8–10 cherry tomatoes, to garnish

SERVES 2–4

1 Skin the fish and cut it into small cubes. Put the cubes into a large bowl and add the ground cumin, mango powder, ground coriander, chilli powder, salt, ginger and cornflour. Mix thoroughly until the fish is well coated.

2 Heat the oil in a deep round-bottomed frying pan or a karahi. Lower the heat slightly and add the fish pieces, three or four at a time. Fry for about 3 minutes, turning constantly. Drain the fish pieces on kitchen paper and transfer to a warmed serving dish. Cover and keep warm while you fry the remaining fish pieces.

3 Fry the peppers in the remaining oil for about 2 minutes. They should still be slightly crisp. Drain on kitchen paper.

4 Add the peppers to the fish and garnish with the cherry tomatoes. Serve immediately with a cucumber and mint raita and parathas, if wished.

BALTI FISH FILLETS IN SPICY COCONUT SAUCE

Use fresh fish fillets to make this dish if you can, as they have much more flavour than frozen ones. Serve with plain boiled rice.

INGREDIENTS
30ml/2 tbsp corn oil
5ml/1 tsp onion seeds
4 dried red chillies
3 garlic cloves, sliced
1 onion, sliced
2 tomatoes, sliced
30ml/2 tbsp desiccated coconut
5ml/1 tsp salt
5ml/1 tsp ground coriander
4 flatfish fillets, such as plaice, sole or flounder, about 75g/3oz each
150ml/¼ pint/⅔ cup water
15ml/1 tbsp lime juice
15ml/1 tbsp chopped fresh coriander

SERVES 4

1 Heat the oil in a deep round-bottomed frying pan or a karahi. Lower the heat slightly and add the onion seeds, dried red chillies, garlic and onion. Cook for about 3–4 minutes, stirring once or twice.

2 Add the tomatoes, coconut, salt and coriander and stir thoroughly to blend with the onion and spices.

3 Cut each fish fillet into three pieces. Drop the fish pieces into the mixture, turn them gently until they are well coated, and cook for 5–7 minutes *(right)*, lowering the heat if necessary.

4 Add the water, lime juice and fresh coriander and cook for 3–5 minutes until the water has almost evaporated.

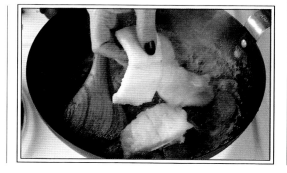

PANEER BALTI WITH PRAWNS

Although paneer is not eaten a great deal in Pakistan, it makes an excellent substitute for red meat. Here, it is combined with king prawns to make a delicious dish.

INGREDIENTS

12 cooked king prawns
175g/6oz paneer
30ml/2 tbsp tomato purée
60ml/4 tbsp Greek yogurt
7.5ml/1½ tsp garam masala
5ml/1 tsp chilli powder
1 garlic clove, crushed
5ml/1 tsp salt
10ml/2 tsp mango powder
5ml/1 tsp ground coriander
115g/4oz/½ cup butter
15ml/1 tbsp corn oil
3 fresh green chillies, chopped
45ml/3 tbsp chopped fresh coriander
150ml/¼ pint/⅔ cup single cream

SERVES 4

1 Peel the king prawns and put them into a bowl. Cut the paneer into 2–2.5cm/¾–1in cubes and place in a separate bowl.

2 Blend the tomato purée, yogurt, garam masala, chilli powder, garlic, salt, mango powder and ground coriander in a bowl and set aside.

3 Melt the butter with the oil in a deep round-bottomed frying pan or a medium karahi. Lower the heat slightly and quickly fry the paneer and prawns for about 2 minutes. Remove with a slotted spoon and drain on kitchen paper.

4 Pour the spice mixture into the fat remaining in the pan and stir-fry for about 1 minute.

5 Add the paneer and prawns and cook for 7–10 minutes, stirring occasionally, until the prawns are heated through.

6 Add the fresh chillies and 30ml/2 tbsp of the coriander, pour in the cream and cook for about 2 minutes. Serve at once, garnished with the remaining coriander.

HOME-MADE PANEER

To make paneer at home, bring 1 litre/1¾ pints/4 cups milk to the boil over a low heat. Add 30ml/2 tbsp lemon juice, stirring continuously and gently until the milk thickens and begins to curdle. Strain the curdled milk through a sieve lined with muslin. Set aside under a heavy weight for about 1½–2 hours to press to a flat shape about 1cm/½in thick.
Make the paneer a day before you plan to use it in a recipe; it will be firmer and easier to handle. Cut and use as required; it will keep for about 1 week in the fridge.

BALTI PRAWNS IN HOT SAUCE

This sizzling prawn dish is cooked in a fiery hot and spicy sauce. Not only does it contain chilli powder, it is made hotter still by the green chillies mixed with the other spices. If the heat is too much for anyone with a delicate palate, the addition of a raita will help to moderate the fiery heat of the chillies.

INGREDIENTS
2 onions, roughly chopped
30ml/2 tbsp tomato purée
5ml/1 tsp ground coriander
1.5ml/¼ tsp turmeric
5ml/1 tsp chilli powder
2 fresh green chillies
45ml/3 tbsp chopped fresh coriander
30ml/2 tbsp lemon juice
5ml/1 tsp salt
45ml/3 tbsp corn oil
16 peeled, cooked king prawns
1 fresh green chilli, chopped (optional)

SERVES 4

1 Put the onions, tomato purée, ground coriander, turmeric, chilli powder, whole green chillies, 30ml/2 tbsp of the fresh coriander, the lemon juice and salt into a food processor. Process for about 1 minute. If the mixture seems too thick, add a little water and process again.

2 Heat the oil in a deep round-bottomed frying pan or a karahi. Add the spice mixture and fry for 3–5 minutes, or until the sauce has thickened slightly.

3 Add the prawns *(right)* and stir-fry quickly over a medium heat until heated through. Transfer to a serving dish and garnish with the remaining fresh coriander and the chopped green chilli, if using.

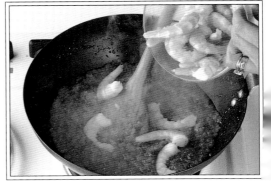

KARAHI PRAWNS AND FENUGREEK

T he black-eyed beans, prawns and paneer make this dish rich in protein, while the combination of both ground and fresh fenugreek add a fragrant and delicious flavour. Use the whole leaves of fresh fenugreek but discard the stalks as they tend to be bitter.

INGREDIENTS
60ml/4 tbsp corn oil
2 onions, sliced
2 tomatoes, sliced
1½ garlic cloves, crushed
5ml/1 tsp chilli powder
5ml/1 tsp grated fresh root ginger
5ml/1 tsp ground cumin
5ml/1 tsp ground coriander
5ml/1 tsp salt
150g/5oz paneer, cubed
5ml/1 tsp ground fenugreek
1 bunch fresh fenugreek, stalks removed
115g/4oz cooked, peeled prawns
2 fresh red chillies, sliced
30ml/2 tbsp chopped fresh coriander
50g/2oz/⅓ cup canned black-eyed beans, drained
15ml/1 tbsp lemon juice

SERVES 4–6

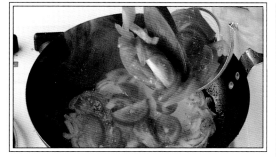

1 Heat the oil in a deep round-bottomed frying pan or a karahi. Lower the heat slightly, add the onions and tomatoes and fry for about 3 minutes.

2 Add the garlic, chilli powder, ginger, ground cumin, ground coriander, salt, paneer and the ground and fresh fenugreek. Lower the heat and stir-fry for about 2 minutes.

3 Add the prawns, red chillies, fresh coriander and the black-eyed beans to the pan and mix well. Cook, stirring occasionally, for a further 3–5 minutes, or until the prawns are heated through. Sprinkle with the lemon juice, transfer to warmed plates, and serve immediately.

SEAFOOD BALTI WITH VEGETABLES

In this dish, the spicy seafood is cooked separately and combined with the vegetables at the end to give a truly delicious combination of flavours.

INGREDIENTS

225g/8oz cod, or any other firm white fish
225g/8oz cooked, peeled prawns
6 crab sticks, halved
15ml/1 tbsp lemon juice
5ml/1 tsp ground coriander
5ml/1 tsp chilli powder
5ml/1 tsp salt
5ml/1 tsp ground cumin
60ml/4 tbsp cornflour
150ml/¼ pint/⅔ cup corn oil
lime slices, to garnish

FOR THE VEGETABLES

150ml/¼ pint/⅔ cup corn oil
2 onions, chopped
5ml/1 tsp onion seeds
½ cauliflower, cut into florets
115g/4oz French beans, cut into
2.5cm/1in lengths
175g/6oz/1 cup sweetcorn
5ml/1 tsp sliced fresh root ginger
5ml/1 tsp each chilli powder and salt
4 fresh green chillies, sliced
30ml/2 tbsp chopped fresh coriander

SERVES 4

1 Skin the fish and cut it into small cubes. Put them into a medium bowl with the prawns and crab sticks and set aside.

2 In a separate bowl, combine the lemon juice, ground coriander, chilli powder, salt and ground cumin. Pour the mixture over the seafood and mix together thoroughly with your hands.

3 Sprinkle with the cornflour and mix again until the seafood is well coated. Cover and leave to marinate in the fridge for about 1 hour for the flavours to develop.

4 To make the vegetable mixture, heat the oil in a deep round-bottomed frying pan. Add the onions and onion seeds and stir-fry for a few minutes until lightly browned.

5 Add the cauliflower, French beans, sweetcorn, ginger, chilli powder, salt, green chillies and fresh coriander and stir-fry for about 7–10 minutes over a moderate heat, making sure that the cauliflower florets retain their shape.

6 Spoon the fried vegetables around the edge of a shallow platter or dish, leaving a space in the middle for the seafood, cover and keep warm.

7 Wash and dry the pan, then heat the oil to fry the seafood. Stir-fry the seafood pieces in 2–3 batches, until golden brown. Remove with a slotted spoon and drain on kitchen paper.

8 Arrange the seafood on the platter or dish in the middle of the vegetables, garnish with the lime slices and serve immediately. Plain boiled rice and raita make ideal accompaniments.

LAMB WITH SPINACH

Lamb with Spinach is a well-known recipe from the Punjab region. It is important to use red peppers as they add such a distinctive flavour to the finished dish.

INGREDIENTS
5ml/1 tsp sliced fresh root ginger
1 garlic clove, crushed
7.5ml/1½ tsp chilli powder
5ml/1 tsp salt
5ml/1 tsp garam masala
90ml/6 tbsp corn oil
2 onions, sliced
675g/1½lb lean lamb, cut into
5cm/2in cubes
600–900ml/1–1½ pints/2½–3¾ cups water
400g/14oz fresh spinach
1 large red pepper, seeded and chopped
3 fresh green chillies, chopped
45ml/3 tbsp chopped fresh coriander
15ml/1 tbsp lemon juice (optional)

SERVES 4–6

COOK'S TIP
Frozen spinach can also be used for this dish, but try to find whole leaf spinach rather than the chopped kind – it has a much better flavour.

1 Mix together the ginger, garlic, chilli powder, salt and garam masala in a bowl. Set aside.

2 Heat the oil in a saucepan, add the onions and fry for 10–12 minutes or until well browned. Add the lamb pieces and stir-fry for about 2 minutes.

3 Add the spice mixture and stir thoroughly until the lamb is well coated. Pour in the water and bring to the boil, then cover the pan and lower the heat. Cook gently for 25–35 minutes without letting the contents of the pan burn. If there is still a lot of water remaining in the pan remove the lid and boil briskly to evaporate the excess.

4 Meanwhile, wash and roughly chop the spinach, discarding any tough stalks, then blanch it for about 1 minute in a pan of boiling water. Drain well.

5 Add the spinach to the lamb and cook for 7–10 minutes, using a wooden spoon in a semi-circular motion, scraping the bottom of the pan as you stir.

6 Add the red pepper, green chillies and chopped fresh coriander to the pan and stir over a moderate heat for 2 minutes. Sprinkle with the lemon juice, if using, and serve immediately. Serve with a simple accompaniment such as plain boiled rice or Naan Bread.

KHARA MASALA LAMB

Whole spices (*khara*) are used in this curry so you should warn your guests. It is delicious with freshly baked Naan Bread or boiled rice.

INGREDIENTS
75ml/5 tbsp corn oil
2 onions, chopped
5ml/1 tsp sliced fresh root ginger
1 garlic clove, sliced
6 dried red chillies
3 cardamom pods
2 cinnamon sticks
6 black peppercorns
3 cloves
2.5ml/½ tsp salt
450g/1lb boned leg of lamb, cubed
600ml/1 pint/2½ cups water
2 fresh green chillies, sliced
30ml/2 tbsp chopped fresh coriander

SERVES 4

COOK'S TIP
The technique of stirring the meat and spices with a semi-circular motion, used in step 3, is called *bhoonoing*. It ensures that the meat is well coated with the spice mixture before the cooking liquid is added.

1 Heat the oil in a large saucepan, lower the heat slightly, add the onions, and fry until they are lightly browned.

2 Add half of the ginger and half of the garlic and stir well. Add half of the red chillies, the cardamom pods, cinnamon, peppercorns, cloves and salt.

3 Add the lamb and fry over a moderate heat. Stir constantly for 5 minutes with a semi-circular movement, using a wooden spoon to scrape the bottom of the pan.

4 Pour in the water, cover with a lid and cook over a moderately low heat for 35–40 minutes, or until the water has evaporated and the meat is tender.

5 Add the remaining ginger, garlic and dried red chillies to the pan, then stir in the fresh green chillies and the chopped fresh coriander.

6 Continue cooking, stirring constantly, until you see some free oil on the sides of the pan. Transfer to a warmed serving dish and serve immediately.

BALTI LAMB TIKKA

This is a traditional tikka recipe, in which the lamb is marinated in yogurt with a mixture of spices. The lamb is usually cut into cubes, but the cooking time can be reduced by half if you cut it into strips instead.

INGREDIENTS
450g/1lb lamb, cut into strips
175ml/6fl oz/¾ cup natural yogurt
5ml/1 tsp ground cumin
5ml/1 tsp ground coriander
5ml/1 tsp chilli powder
1 garlic clove, crushed
5ml/1 tsp salt
5ml/1 tsp garam masala
30ml/2 tbsp chopped fresh coriander
30ml/2 tbsp lemon juice
30ml/2 tbsp corn oil
15ml/1 tbsp tomato purée
1 large green pepper, seeded and sliced
3 large fresh red chillies

SERVES 4

1 Put the lamb strips, yogurt, ground cumin, ground coriander, chilli powder, garlic, salt, garam masala, fresh coriander and lemon juice into a large bowl and stir thoroughly. Cover and set aside for at least 1 hour to marinate.

2 Heat the oil in a deep round-bottomed frying pan or a karahi. Lower the heat slightly and add the tomato purée.

3 Add the lamb strips to the pan, a few at a time, leaving any excess marinade behind in the bowl. Cook the lamb, stirring frequently, for 7–10 minutes, or until it is well browned.

4 Add the green pepper slices and the whole red chillies. Heat through, checking that the lamb is thoroughly cooked, then serve immediately.

BALTI MINCED LAMB WITH POTATOES AND FENUGREEK

The combination of lamb with fresh fenugreek works very well in this dish, which is quite delicious accompanied by plain boiled rice and mango pickle. Use only the fenugreek leaves, as the stalks can be rather bitter.

INGREDIENTS
450g/1lb lean minced lamb
5ml/1 tsp sliced fresh root ginger
1 garlic clove, crushed
7.5ml/1½ tsp chilli powder
5ml/1 tsp salt
1.5ml/¼ tsp turmeric
45ml/3 tbsp corn oil
2 onions, sliced
2 potatoes, parboiled and roughly diced
1 bunch fresh fenugreek, stalks removed
2 tomatoes, chopped
50g/2oz/½ cup frozen peas
30ml/2 tbsp chopped fresh coriander
3 fresh red chillies, seeded and sliced,
to garnish

SERVES 4

1 Put the minced lamb, ginger, garlic, chilli powder, salt and turmeric into a large bowl and mix thoroughly. Set aside.

2 Heat the oil in a deep round-bottomed frying pan. Add the onions and fry for about 5 minutes until golden brown.

3 Add the spiced minced lamb to the onions and stir-fry over a moderate heat for 5–7 minutes.

4 Stir in the potatoes, fenugreek leaves, tomatoes and peas and cook for a further 5–7 minutes, stirring constantly.

5 Just before serving, stir in the chopped fresh coriander and garnish with the fresh red chillies.

BALTI MINI LAMB KEBABS WITH BABY ONIONS

This is rather an unusual Balti dish as the kebabs are grilled before being added to the karahi for the final stage of cooking.

INGREDIENTS
450g/1lb lean minced lamb
1 onion, finely chopped
5ml/1 tsp garam masala
1 garlic clove, crushed
2 fresh green chillies, finely chopped
30ml/2 tbsp chopped fresh coriander
5ml/1 tsp salt
15ml/1 tbsp plain flour
60ml/4 tbsp corn oil
12 baby onions
4 fresh green chillies, sliced
12 cherry tomatoes
30ml/2 tbsp chopped fresh
coriander, to garnish

SERVES 6

1 Blend the minced lamb, onion, garam masala, garlic, green chillies, fresh coriander, salt and flour in a bowl. Use your hands to make sure that all the ingredients are thoroughly mixed together.

2 Transfer the mixture to a food processor and process for about 1 minute, to make the mixture finer in texture.

3 Return the mixture to the bowl. Break off small pieces, about the size of a lime, and wrap them around skewers to form small sausage shapes. Put about two mini kebabs on each skewer.

4 Baste the kebabs with 15ml/1 tbsp of the oil and place under a preheated hot grill for 12–15 minutes, turning and basting occasionally, until they are evenly browned.

5 Heat the remaining oil in a deep round-bottomed frying pan or a medium karahi. Lower the heat slightly and add the baby onions. As soon as they start to colour, add the green chillies and tomatoes.

6 Remove the mini kebabs from their skewers and add them to the onion and tomato mixture. Stir gently for about 3 minutes to heat them through.

7 Transfer to a warmed serving dish and garnish with fresh coriander. Serve with Spicy Balti Potatoes and parathas.

LAMB CHOPS KASHMIRI-STYLE

T hese chops are cooked in a unique way, being first boiled in milk and then fried. Despite the many spices, this dish has a mild flavour, and is delicious served with fried rice and a lentil dish.

INGREDIENTS
8–12 lamb chops, about
50–75g/2–3oz each
2.5cm/1in piece cinnamon stick
1 bay leaf
2.5ml/½ tsp fennel seeds
2.5ml/½ tsp black peppercorns
3 green cardamom pods
5ml/1 tsp salt
600ml/1 pint/2½ cups milk
150ml/¼ pint/⅔ cup evaporated milk
150ml/¼ pint/⅔ cup natural yogurt
30ml/2 tbsp plain flour
5ml/1 tsp chilli powder
5ml/1 tsp fresh root ginger
2.5ml/½ tsp garam masala
1 garlic clove, crushed
pinch of salt
300ml/½ pint/1¼ cups corn oil
mint sprigs and lime quarters, to garnish

SERVES 4

1 Trim the lamb chops and place them in a saucepan with the cinnamon, bay leaf, fennel seeds, peppercorns, cardamom, salt and milk. Bring to the boil over a high heat.

2 Lower the heat and cook the chops for 12–15 minutes, or until the milk has reduced by half. Add the evaporated milk and simmer until the chops are cooked and the milk has almost completely reduced.

3 While the chops are cooking, blend the yogurt, flour, chilli powder, ginger, garam masala, garlic and a pinch of salt in a bowl.

4 Remove the chops from the pan and discard the whole spices. Add the chops to the spicy yogurt mixture.

5 Heat the oil in a deep round-bottomed frying pan or a karahi. Lower the heat slightly, add the chops and fry until golden brown, turning them once or twice as they cook so they are fried evenly.

6 Transfer the chops to a warmed serving dish, garnish with the mint sprigs and lime quarters, and serve at once.

LENTILS WITH LAMB AND TOMATOES

This aromatically spiced dish is rich in protein and has a deliciously light texture. Colourful Pullao Rice makes a perfect accompaniment.

INGREDIENTS
60ml/4 tbsp corn oil
2 bay leaves
2 cloves
4 black peppercorns
1 onion, sliced
450g/1lb lean lamb, boned and cubed
1.5ml/¼ tsp ground turmeric
7.5ml/1½ tsp chilli powder
5ml/1 tsp crushed coriander seeds
2.5cm/1in piece cinnamon stick
1 garlic clove, crushed
7.5ml/1½ tsp salt
1.5 litres/2½ pints/6¼ cups water
50g/2oz/⅓ cup chana dhal (split yellow lentils) or yellow split peas
2 tomatoes, quartered
2 fresh green chillies, chopped
15ml/1 tbsp chopped fresh coriander

SERVES 4

1 Heat the oil in a deep round-bottomed frying pan or a karahi. Lower the heat slightly and add the bay leaves, cloves, peppercorns and onion and fry for about 5 minutes, or until the onions are golden.

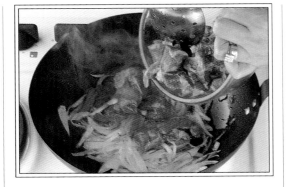

2 Add the lamb cubes, ground turmeric, chilli powder, coriander seeds, cinnamon stick, garlic and most of the salt to the pan. Stir-fry the lamb mixture for about 5 minutes over a moderate heat.

3 Pour in 900ml/1½ pints/3¾ cups of the water and cover the pan with a lid or foil, making sure the foil does not come into contact with the contents of the pan. Simmer the lamb over a low heat for about 35–40 minutes, or until the water has evaporated and the lamb is tender.

4 Meanwhile, put the lentils into a saucepan with the remaining 600ml/1 pint/2½ cups water and boil for about 12–15 minutes, or until the water has almost evaporated and the lentils are soft enough to mash easily. If the lentil mixture is too thick, gradually add up to 150ml/¼ pint/⅔ cup water until they mash easily.

5 When the lamb is tender, stir-fry the mixture using a wooden spoon, until some free oil begins to appear on the sides of the pan.

6 Add the cooked lentils to the lamb and mix together well with a wooden spoon.

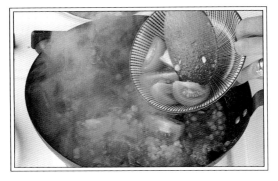

7 Stir in the tomatoes, chillies and fresh coriander then transfer to a warmed serving dish and serve immediately.

VARIATION
Boned and cubed chicken can be used in place of the lamb. At step 3, reduce the amount of water to 300ml/½ pint/1¼ cups and cook uncovered, stirring occasionally, for 10–15 minutes or until the water has evaporated and the chicken is cooked through.

BALTI BABY VEGETABLES

There is a wide selection of baby vegetables available these days, and this simple recipe does full justice to their delicate flavour.

INGREDIENTS
10 new potatoes, halved
12–14 baby carrots
12–14 baby courgettes
30ml/2 tbsp corn oil
15 baby onions
30ml/2 tbsp chilli sauce
1 garlic clove, crushed
5ml/1 tsp grated fresh root ginger
400g/14oz/2 cups canned
chick-peas, drained
10 cherry tomatoes
salt
5ml/1 tsp crushed dried red chillies and
30ml/2 tbsp sesame seeds, to garnish

SERVES 4–6

VARIATION
By varying the vegetables and making different combinations, this recipe can form the basis for a wide variety of accompaniments. Try baby sweetcorn, French beans, mange-tout, okra and cauliflower florets.

1 Bring a pan of salted water to the boil and add the potatoes and carrots. After about 12–15 minutes, add the courgettes and boil for a further 5 minutes, or until all the vegetables are just tender. Drain well and set aside.

2 Heat the oil in a deep round-bottomed frying pan or a karahi, add the baby onions and fry until golden brown. Lower the heat and add the chilli sauce, garlic, ginger and 5ml/1 tsp salt, taking care not to let the mixture burn.

3 Add the chick-peas and stir-fry over a moderate heat until all the moisture has been absorbed.

4 Add the cooked vegetables and cherry tomatoes and stir with a slotted spoon for about 2 minutes until heated through.

5 Transfer to a warmed serving dish, garnish with the crushed red chillies and sesame seeds and serve immediately.

SPICED POTATOES AND CARROTS PARISIENNE

P arisienne vegetables are root vegetables that have been peeled and cut into perfectly spherical shapes. They are available ready prepared in some supermarkets. This dish looks fresh and appetizing and tastes delicious.

INGREDIENTS
175g/6oz carrots parisienne
175g/6oz potatoes parisienne
115g/4oz runner beans, sliced
75g/3oz/6 tbsp butter
15ml/1 tbsp corn oil
1.5ml/¼ tsp onion seeds
1.5ml/¼ tsp fenugreek seeds
4 dried red chillies
2.5ml/½ tsp mustard seeds
6 curry leaves
1 onion, sliced
5ml/1 tsp salt
4 garlic cloves, sliced
4 fresh red chillies
15ml/1 tbsp chopped fresh coriander
15ml/1 tbsp chopped fresh mint
mint sprig, to garnish

SERVES 4

1 Put the carrots, potatoes and runner beans into a pan of boiling water and cook for about 7 minutes, or until they are just tender. Drain and set aside.

2 Heat the butter with the oil in a deep round-bottomed frying pan or a large karahi and add the onion seeds, fenugreek seeds, dried red chillies, mustard seeds and curry leaves and cook for 1 minute. Add the onion and fry for 3–5 minutes, stirring and turning constantly, until it is thoroughly coated with the spice mixture.

3 Add the salt, garlic and fresh chillies, then the cooked carrots, potatoes and runner beans, and stir gently, over a moderate heat for about 5 minutes.

4 Stir in the fresh coriander and mint, transfer to a warmed serving dish and serve hot, garnished with a sprig of mint.

KARAHI SHREDDED CABBAGE WITH CUMIN

T his cabbage dish is only lightly spiced and makes a good accompaniment to most other Balti and western dishes.

INGREDIENTS
15ml/1 tbsp corn oil
50g/2oz/4 tbsp butter
2.5ml/½ tsp crushed coriander seeds
2.5ml/½ tsp white cumin seeds
6 dried red chillies
1 small Savoy cabbage, shredded
12 mange-touts
12 baby sweetcorn
3 fresh red chillies, seeded and sliced
salt, to taste
25g/1oz/¼ cup flaked almonds, toasted
and 15ml/1 tbsp chopped fresh
coriander, to garnish

SERVES 4

1 Heat the oil with the butter in a deep round-bottomed frying pan or a karahi. When it is hot, add the crushed coriander seeds, white cumin seeds and dried red chillies and stir-fry for 1 minute.

2 Add the shredded cabbage and mange-touts and stir-fry for about 5 minutes.

3 Add the baby sweetcorn, chillies *(right)*, and salt and fry for 3 minutes, until the vegetables are tender.

4 Garnish with the toasted almonds and fresh coriander, and serve hot.

BALTI STUFFED VEGETABLES

ubergines and peppers make a good combination. Here they are stuffed with an aromatic lamb filling.

INGREDIENTS
3 small aubergines
1 each red, green and yellow pepper

FOR THE STUFFING
45ml/3 tbsp corn oil
3 onions, sliced
5ml/1 tsp chilli powder
1.5ml/¼ tsp turmeric
5ml/1 tsp ground coriander
5ml/1 tsp ground cumin
1 garlic clove, crushed
5ml/1 tsp salt
450g/1lb lean minced lamb
30ml/2 tbsp chopped fresh coriander

FOR THE SAUTEED ONIONS
45ml/3 tbsp corn oil
5ml/1 tsp mixed onion, mustard,
fenugreek and white cumin seeds
4 dried red chillies
3 onions, roughly chopped
5ml/1 tsp salt
2 tomatoes, sliced
2 fresh green chillies, chopped
30ml/2 tbsp chopped fresh coriander

SERVES 6

1 Prepare the vegetables. Slit the aubergines lengthways up to the stalks, leaving the stalks intact. Cut the tops off the peppers and scoop out the seeds. You can keep the pepper tops to use as 'lids' for the stuffed vegetables, if wished.

2 To make the stuffing, heat the oil in a saucepan. Add the onions and fry for about 3 minutes. Lower the heat and add the chilli powder, turmeric, ground coriander, ground cumin, garlic and salt, and stir-fry for about 1 minute. Add the minced lamb and turn up the heat.

3 Stir-fry for 7–10 minutes, or until the mince is cooked. Add the fresh coriander towards the end of the cooking time and stir to mix. Remove the mince mixture from the heat, cover and set aside.

4 Make the sautéed onions. Heat the oil in a deep round-bottomed frying pan or a karahi and add the mixed onion, mustard, fenugreek and white cumin seeds and red chillies and fry for 1 minute. Add the onions and fry for 2 minutes or until soft.

5 Add the salt, sliced tomatoes, chopped green chillies and the chopped fresh coriander and cook for 1 further minute. Remove from the heat and set aside.

6 When the minced lamb mixture is cool, stuff the aubergines and peppers. Using a small spoon, fill them quite loosely with the meat mixture.

7 Place the stuffed vegetables on top of the sautéed onions in the karahi. Cover with foil, making sure the foil doesn't touch the food, and cook over a low heat for about 15 minutes, until the aubergines and peppers are tender. Serve with a dish of plain boiled rice or Colourful Pullao Rice.

COOK'S TIP
Large beef tomatoes are also delicious stuffed with this lightly spiced lamb mixture. Simply cut off the tops and scoop out the cores, seeds and some of the pulp and cook as above.

SPICY BALTI POTATOES

his spice mixture transforms new potatoes into an exotic vegetable. Vary the spices to suit your taste.

INGREDIENTS
45ml/3 tbsp corn oil
2.5ml/½ tsp white cumin seeds
5ml/1 tsp crushed dried red chillies
2.5ml/½ tsp mixed onion, mustard and fenugreek seeds
2.5ml/½ tsp fennel seeds
3 garlic cloves
2.5ml/½ tsp sliced fresh root ginger
2 onions, sliced
6 new potatoes, cut into 5mm/¼in slices
15ml/1 tbsp chopped fresh coriander
1 fresh red chilli, seeded and sliced

SERVES 4

1 Heat the oil in a deep round-bottomed frying pan. Lower the heat slightly and add the cumin seeds, red chillies, mixed onion, mustard and fenugreek seeds, fennel seeds, garlic and ginger. Fry for 1 minute, then add the onions and fry for 5 minutes.

2 Add the potatoes, fresh coriander and red chilli, mix well, and cover tightly. Cook over a very low heat for about 7 minutes. Remove the foil and serve hot.

OKRA WITH GREEN MANGO AND LENTILS

f you like okra, you'll love this spicy and tangy dish. Use canned okra if you cannot find the fresh variety.

INGREDIENTS
115g/4oz/⅔ cup split yellow lentils
45ml/3 tbsp corn oil
2.5ml/½ tsp onion seeds
2 onions, sliced
2.5ml/½ tsp ground fenugreek
5ml/1 tsp sliced fresh root ginger
1 garlic clove, crushed
7.5ml/1½ tsp chilli powder
1.5ml/¼ tsp turmeric
5ml/1 tsp ground coriander
1 green mango, peeled and sliced
450g/1lb okra, cut into 2.5cm/1in pieces
7.5ml/1½ tsp salt
2 fresh red chillies, seeded and sliced
30ml/2 tbsp chopped fresh coriander
1 tomato, sliced

SERVES 4

1 Wash the lentils thoroughly and put them into a saucepan with enough water to cover. Bring to the boil and cook for about 30 minutes until soft but not mushy. Drain and set aside.

2 Heat the oil in a deep round-bottomed frying pan or a karahi and fry the onion seeds until they begin to pop. Add the onions and fry until golden brown. Lower the heat and add the ground fenugreek, ginger, garlic, chilli powder, turmeric and ground coriander.

3 Add the mango slices and the okra. Stir well, add the salt, red chillies and fresh coriander and stir-fry for about 3 minutes, or until the okra is well cooked.

4 Add the cooked lentils and sliced tomato and cook for a further 3 minutes. Serve immediately.

Spicy Balti Potatoes (TOP) and Okra with Green Mango and Lentils

NAAN BREAD

There are many ways of making naan bread, but this method is particularly easy to follow. Naans should be served warm, preferably straight from the grill.

INGREDIENTS

5ml/1 tsp caster sugar
5ml/1 tsp easy-blend dried yeast
150ml/¼ pint/⅔ cup warm water
225g/8oz/2 cups plain flour, plus extra
for dusting
5ml/1 tsp salt
50g/2oz/4 tbsp unsalted
butter, melted
5ml/1 tsp ghee, melted
5ml/1 tsp onion seeds

MAKES ABOUT 6

COOK'S TIP
Poppy seeds or fresh chopped coriander make an equally delicious topping instead of the onion seeds.

1 Put the sugar and yeast into a small bowl and add the warm water. Mix well with a small spoon until the yeast has dissolved, and set aside for about 10 minutes, or until the mixture is frothy.

2 Place the flour in a large bowl, make a well in the middle and add the salt, melted butter and the yeast mixture.

3 Mix well to form a smooth ball of dough, using your hands, and adding a little more water if the dough is too dry. Take care not to add too much water.

4 Turn out the dough on to a lightly floured surface and knead for about 5 minutes, or until smooth.

5 Return the dough to the bowl, cover with clear film and leave in a warm place for about 1½ hours, or until doubled in size.

6 Turn out the dough again on to a lightly floured surface and knead for a further 2 minutes until smooth.

7 Break off small pieces of the dough with your hands, and roll into rounds about 13cm/5in in diameter and 1cm/½in thick.

8 Place the naans on a sheet of greased foil under a preheated very hot grill for about 7–10 minutes, turning twice and brushing with ghee and sprinkling with onion seeds. Serve immediately if possible, or keep wrapped in foil until required.

COLOURFUL PULLAO RICE

his lightly spiced rice makes a very attractive accompaniment to many Balti dishes.

INGREDIENTS
450g/1lb/2 cups basmati rice
75g/3oz/6 tbsp unsalted butter
4 cloves
4 green cardamom pods
2 bay leaves
5ml/1 tsp salt
1 litre/1¾ pints/4 cups water
few drops each of yellow, green and red food colouring

SERVES 4–6

1 Wash the rice twice to remove any grit, drain and set aside in a bowl.

2 Melt the butter in a saucepan, then add the cloves, cardamoms, bay leaves and salt. Lower the heat and add the rice. Fry for about 1 minute, stirring constantly. Add the water and bring to the boil. As soon as it has boiled, cover the pan and reduce the heat. Cook for 15–20 minutes.

3 Just before serving, pour a few drops of each food colouring into different parts of the pan. Leave to stand, covered, for 5 minutes, mix gently and serve.

FRUITY PULLAO

his is a lovely way to cook rice and goes very well with all meat dishes, especially lamb.

INGREDIENTS
450g/1lb/2 cups basmati rice
75g/3oz/6 tbsp unsalted butter
15ml/1 tbsp corn oil
2 bay leaves
6 black peppercorns
4 green cardamom pods
5ml/1 tsp salt
75g/3oz/½ cup sultanas
50g/2oz/½ cup flaked almonds
1 litre/1¾ pint/4 cups water

SERVES 4–6

COOK'S TIP
Turmeric colours rice yellow. Add 1.5–2.5ml/¼–½ tsp to the boiling water before adding the rice.

1 Wash the rice twice to remove any grit, drain and set aside in a sieve while you prepare and cook the spices.

2 Heat the butter with the oil in a saucepan. Lower the heat and add the bay leaves, peppercorns and cardamom pods, and fry for about 30 seconds.

3 Add the rice, salt, sultanas and flaked almonds, stir-fry for about 1 minute, then pour in the water. Bring to the boil, then cover with a tightly-fitting lid and lower the heat. Cook for 15–20 minutes.

4 Turn off the heat and leave the rice to stand, still covered, for about 5 minutes before serving.

Colourful Pullao Rice (TOP) and Fruity Pullao

APRICOT CHUTNEY

TASTY TOASTS

Chutneys add zest to most meals, and in Pakistan you will find a selection of different kinds served in tiny bowls for people to choose from.

These crunchy toasts make an ideal snack or part of a brunch. They are especially delicious served with grilled tomatoes and baked beans.

INGREDIENTS
450g/1lb/3 cups dried apricots,
finely diced
5ml/1 tsp garam masala
275g/10oz/1¼ cups soft light brown sugar
5ml/1 tsp sliced fresh root ginger
5ml/1 tsp salt
75g/3oz/½ cup sultanas
450ml/¾ pint/scant 2 cups malt vinegar
450ml/¾ pint/scant 2 cups water

MAKES ABOUT 450G/1LB

INGREDIENTS
4 eggs
300ml/½ pint/1¼ cups milk
2 fresh green chillies, finely chopped
30ml/2 tbsp chopped fresh coriander
75g/3oz Cheddar or mozzarella
cheese, grated
2.5ml/½ tsp salt
1.5ml/¼ tsp freshly ground black pepper
4 slices bread
corn oil, for frying

MAKES 8

1 Put the dried apricots, garam masala, light brown sugar, ginger, salt, sultanas, vinegar and water into a saucepan and mix together thoroughly.

2 Bring to the boil, then turn down the heat and simmer for 30–35 minutes, stirring occasionally.

3 When the chutney has thickened to a fairly stiff consistency, transfer to 2–3 sterilized glass jars and leave to cool. This chutney should be stored in the fridge.

VARIATION
If you have any leftover naan bread or parathas, cut into pieces and use instead of the slices of bread. For a milder version, omit the chillies and replace with finely chopped green pepper.

1 Break the eggs into a bowl and whisk together. Slowly add the milk and whisk again. Add the chillies, fresh coriander, cheese, salt and pepper.

2 Cut the bread slices in half diagonally, and dip them, one at a time, into the egg and spice mixture.

3 Heat the oil in a medium frying pan and fry the bread slices over a moderate heat, turning them once or twice, until they are golden brown.

4 Using a fish slice to drain off any excess oil, remove the toasts from the pan and serve immediately.

Apricot Chutney (TOP) and Tasty Toasts

INDEX